The Adventures of
Sweet Petite

SHERI DUNAWAY

Illustrated by: **Terry Hahn**

WestBow Press books may be ordered through booksellers or by contacting:

WestBow Press
A Division of Thomas Nelson & Zondervan
1663 Liberty Drive
Bloomington, IN 47403
www.westbowpress.com
844-714-3454

All Scripture quotations are taken from the New King James and International Children's Bible Version.
Copyright © 1982 by Thomas Nelson, Inc. Used by permission. All rights reserved.

ISBN: 979-8-3850-1444-6 (sc)
ISBN: 979-8-3850-1445-3 (hc)
ISBN: 979-8-3850-1446-0 (e)

Library of Congress Control Number: 2023923925

Print information available on the last page.

WestBow Press rev. date: 04/26/2024

WESTBOW
P R E S S®
A DIVISION OF THOMAS NELSON
& ZONDERVAN

Contents

THE ADVENTURES OF SWEET PETITE - DEDICATION TO BILLY CLAY DUNAWAY

This book - that depicts the joy of an encounter with one of God's precious creatures - I dedicate to my nephew, Billy Clay. Billy, your love and example of overcoming some of life's greatest trials have been a constant strength to me and my family. We love you deeply!

Chapter 1

Little Bird Be Brave - You're About To Be Saved!

...not even one little bird can die without your Father's knowledge. God even knows how many hairs are on your head. You are worth much more than many birds.
(Matthew 10:29-31-ICB)

Baby blue jay on the ground, fallen, helpless—will you be found?
Just a baby—you can't even see! Surely Mama
Bird is thinking, *Where can she be?*
She might be in danger. Oh me, oh my! I
haven't yet taught her how to fly.
You can do nothing but lie there alone; you
think your mama bird has flown.
She's thinking you're lost and can't be found,
baby blue jay on the ground.
God knows when even a sparrow falls, and
He knows you've fallen too.

But look! One of His own is close by and
just happens to be watching you.
She is watching to help you. She knows you cannot fly.
And she's waiting, to be sure Mama
Bird isn't somewhere close by.
Knowing you must be safe from the heat
as the summer sun beats down
on your tiny helpless body, as you lie there on the ground.
But there is no hope to get back, no
hope to return to the others,
for you Sweet Petite to rejoin your mama, sisters, and brothers.

Then a voice you hear, speaking softly and sweet.
Is it Mama Bird? "Tweet, tweet, tweet, tweet!"
Make sure she hears; sing as loudly as you can; tweet,
tweet, little blue jay—tweet, tweet again!
You're no longer afraid; you know it's her! It's
your mommy; she came back for this bird!
She's holding you, carrying you; you know you're now
safe. Mommy is getting you out of this place.

I was hungry, and you fed me. I was thirsty, and you gave me a drink. I was alone, and you invited me into your home.
(Matthew 25:35-ICB)

You don't understand because you can't see; you don't
understand it's your "new mommy."
For one of God's own has taken you in, back to her nest and her children.
This "people mommy" is now yours too. Her nest is a house, but it's now home for you.
Her nest is big; it has walls and a roof. It's cool and comfy, with a dog that goes *woof* !
You're wondering what's going on? And you wish that you could see.

You're just not sure, not sure at all about this new family.
Once you can see, though, things will change, but for
now to you your life seems really strange.
But you're home and loved; it's the end of your plight.
You and mommy, together… nighty-night.

**Sometimes we need to "live by what we believe,
not by what we can see."
(II Corinthians 5:7-ICB)**

Walking by faith, not by sight.

Chapter 2
Welcome Little One To Our Happy Home

Trust the Lord with all your heart. Don't depend on your own understanding. Remember the Lord in everything you do. And He will help you go the right way. (Proverbs 3:5-6-ICB)

Five days pass and you open your eyes. My, are you in for a big surprise!
Here they are, your new family---Woof, brother, sister and your new "people mommy".

Now you can see them and their dog that goes *woof*.
Indeed, all is different under this roof.
No feathers, no wings, Mom's not even blue! And she doesn't chirp or tweet like you do.
Well, none of that matters, this is now your nest; you'll
just have to deal with all of the rest.
And though it's different, it's mostly good, even though
they don't look like you thought they would.
They open their lips; it's words they speak. You chirp
and sing, and it comes from a beak.

Pooch says *woof*, and that's about it. Sometimes you sure do wish he would quit!
He's big and furry with a black nose and eyes. But you have a feeling his bark's a disguise.
You think even though he's scary at first, his bark, from his bite, is definitely worse.
Who knows? Maybe there's hope for him yet. And you're pretty sure he is no threat.

He wags his tail all the time, and you're thinking that is an excellent sign.
You're pretty sure that he's saying, "Hi! Happy you're here, glad you stopped by!"

eet!
tweet!

8

petite

They're kind and gentle, and they saved your life; yes,
they saved you during your time of strife.
So woof, chirp, or words, humans or blue, they
know your *tweet* means "I love you."
They know you're thankful for all they have done;
for this little blue jay, a new life has begun.
They all have names, so they gave you one too.

Hi **Sweet Petite**! **How do you do!**

From your nest to the ground, on that day you fell down;
from the ground to a box on a soft white sock.
From the box, now hopping is all you can do, but
it's the beginning of a new life for you.

**My children, our love should not be only words...our love
must be true love. And we show that love by what we do.
(1 John 3:18-ICB)**

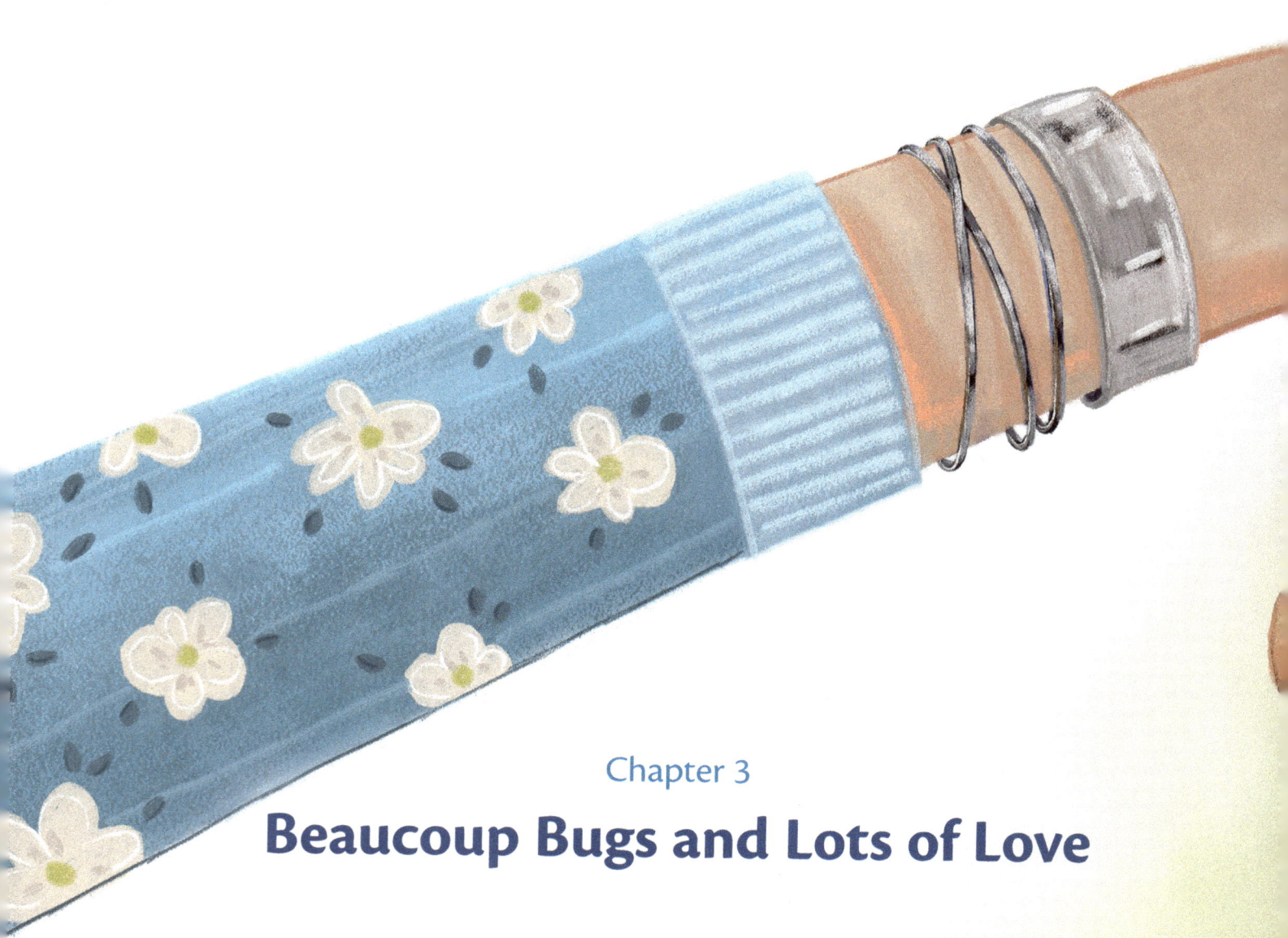

Chapter 3

Beaucoup Bugs and Lots of Love

**Do for other people the same things
you want them to do for you.
(Matthew 7:12-ICB)**

You're getting hungry, and eager to eat. You'll
let them know with a loud *tweet, tweet.*
You're sure ready for something good—now if someone
would just kindly bring you some food!
Soon you know Mommy will bring you a bug
or a worm or maybe a fat, juicy slug!
Mmmm. Yummy! You want another. Uh, do you
have to share with sister and brother?

12

You're getting bigger and bigger each day. You're
growing stronger, and you love to play!
Soon enough, you are able to stand, and as you get
stronger, you can perch on mommy's hand.
Stronger and stronger, you grow as you should,
looking more beautiful, as she knew you would.
She can tell by your song you're ready to get to
your first time out and upcoming debut.

This upcoming debut will be in the sky, the
day you take wing and are ready to fly.
Now stretching your wings and learning to fly, but
these walls and ceiling make it hard to go high.
Your favorite thing is being outside, sitting
on your cage, looking up at the sky.

Now Mommy thinks the time is here to venture your flight outside in the air.
You take off from your cage, here you go, and find it easy if you just fly low.
But each day you get better and don't fall to the ground. You're
almost there, to the trees where you're bound.
Mommy looks on and laughs and smiles. Behind you now are the worst of your trials.
You and Woof are now friends true. It doesn't matter if he's not blue, has
no feathers, and he can't fly; he has no wings, that's probably why!
He doesn't eat bugs, but that's a blessing;
you don't have to share—and that's a good thing!
He has a big nose, enough for two; and when it comes to singing, he doesn't have a clue!
He can't chirp or tweet; he just *woofs* all day long. Hush
up, Woof! Petite's trying to sing her song!

— woof! woof!

Still, every day you have such fun. You fly low, while on the ground he runs. You fly just above; he follows below—barking, of course, wherever you go.

You can see yourself someday perched out on a limb, up high in a tree, you and him. Hmm. Maybe that's not a bright idea after all. Woof, might break the branch and fall! He's rather big, I'm sure you'd agree. He might look silly on a branch in a tree!

Dear friends, we should love each other, because love comes from God. The person who loves has become God's child and knows God. (1 John 4:7-ICB)

Chapter 4

Debut In The Blue

Then God said, "let birds fly in the air above the earth." He made every bird that flies. God saw that this was good. God blessed them and said, "Have many young ones and grow in number, on the earth." (Genesis 1:20-23-ICB)

Now you're in full costume, in feathers of blue;
it's almost time to bid this life adieu.
Beauty as compared with lilies of the field—your
beauty is striking, now completely revealed.
So let's get started; now give it a try. Let's rehearse for your
final goodbye. No more flying low for you—it's up to the
trees; up into the blue. You must fly away and live with the
others, to go find "bird mommy", sisters, and brothers.

You got your start inside four walls, but your instincts
tell you another life calls. You've flown low and had
adventures with Woof, but now the goal is up to
the roof! Then from the roof, go fly to the trees, to
the sky, to the birds, your face in the breeze.

This is the day the LORD has made;
We will rejoice and be glad in it!
(Psalms 118:24-NKJV)

Off you go, and it does take a while to get
high enough and to do it with style.
But soon enough you fly like a pro; you
can fly high, or you can fly low.
You can land on a branch, on the roof, or the ground,
and for you, Sweet Petite, you're heaven bound.

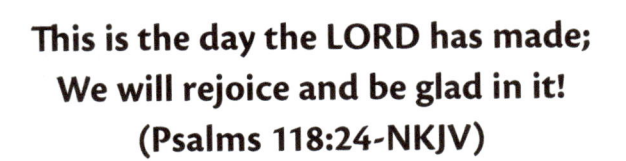

Flying with confidence, flying with grace, and if
birds can smile, there is one on your face!
You're one happy birdie doing your thing. You
wish Mommy and Woof had wings!
Then they could go with you anywhere, and this
exciting time with them you could share.
But there are many other birds all around; you
follow them to see where they're bound.
You see other Woofs and Mommies below; there are more homes
and roofs the farther you go. What a day for you this has been to
fly with birds, now becoming your new friends. The beauty of the
sky, the trees, the sun, and bugs everywhere—boy, this is fun!

petite
petite!!!

My, my, uh-oh! Where'd the time go? You've been gone
so long; where's your home? You do not know!
You want to go home, but you don't know the way.
The sun is setting; it's the end of the day.
Maybe Mommy thinks you're not coming back.
You've never been out when the sky is black.
It's just like before; you're all alone. And once again your Mommy is gone.
But wait! Again, do her voice you hear? "Petite,
Petite!" That's your Mommy dear!
She's calling louder, she hears your tweet. She knows
you're coming back, not quite ready to leave.
In the days ahead, you'll get braver, but for right now, with her you feel safer.

**"I am the Lord your God.
I teach you to do what is good.
I lead you in the way you should go."
(Isaiah 48:17-ICB)**

29

Chapter 5

Tickety-Boo! God Loves You!

**Lord, I trust you. I have said, "You are my God.
My life is in your hands." (Psalms 31:14-15-ICB)**

Mommy's thinking about the future and what it's going to bring….a
future you've not thought of Petite, a future you've yet to see.
So exciting, everything new—green trees to perch on, endless sky of blue. You're
so happy just being out there. How wonderful it is for Mommy to share
this adventure you're about to begin—or is this the
beginning of what is to become the end?
Let's not think about it; and anyway, who knows?
Maybe you will stay; maybe you won't go.
But whatever happens, for you what is best; just raising you, Mommy feels so blessed.
To you, she is Mommy; she nurtured and raised you, fed
you, loved you, picked you up, and saved you.
But there are other birds out there; as now you have seen.
And with them is where you need to be.
She must help you go there. She knows you can do it. It's
why God gave you wings; there'll be nothing to it!

For this is who you are, Petite, a beautiful blue jay,
now go and meet, with others like you, flying free.
It's time to go; it's time to leave Mommy.
You learn how to fly like all your kind, and you
fly each day, leaving Mommy behind,
never sure if you'll return, but first in her heart, you are her
concern. For you, little blue bird, to be happy and safe—for
you, little blue bird, to be in your place. Your home is no longer
living with Mommy, and your life is finally where it should be.
Like it or not, Mommy has no doubt, and so however this
story turns out, Sweet Petite you are what it is all about.

Chapter 6

Tweet, Tweet! Bonjour Petite!

His compassions fail not.
***They are* new every morning;**
Great is Your faithfulness.
(Lamentations 3:22-23 NKJV)

Each day you come to visit Mommy. You get
her attention with your usual tweet.
In the mornings you call "*Tweet, tweet*—get up!
Come and bring me my fruit and my nuts!"

How grand it is to have such a friend; every day
is a joy, Mommy doesn't want it to end.
You're free to go wherever you will, but you
choose to come and see Mommy still.
You have your freedom; she has such delight. She wonders,
"can't it just go on like this? Wouldn't that be all right?"
"Petite, Petite," she calls to you, hoping
each day you've not left for good.
Swooping down, you land upon her head. She holds
out her hand and says, "Please perch here instead!"

"Bonjour, Petite!" She's happy to see you; as you're
pecking her Bible, pecking her "tenny" shoes.
Yes, just about anything in your reach,
anything you can pick up with your beak!
She brings you a mirror, a bell, and some
bling. You are delighted with everything.
She sets them outside on the table
for you, and says "with these you
may do whatever you want to."
You pick them up with your beak one by one
and carry them away till they are all gone.
Then you take her glasses and with them fly away.
She stands up to chase you, shouting out, "Hey!
Give me those glasses, you naughty bird!
Birds don't need glasses; that's absurd!"
She laughs and you know it's all a game;
but her glasses you keep all the same.

She speaks to you as you're perched on her hand; and
you look into her eyes as if to say you understand.
Maybe it's possible that you do.
After all, God the Creator made both of you.

**God will yet fill your mouth with laughter. And he
will fill your lips with shouts of joy. (Job 8:21-ICB)**

**God is happy when we consider others over
ourselves, and what is best for them. Love
is not selfish. (I Corinthians 13:5-ICB)**

Chapter 7

Your True Love Is Up Above

For You have been a strength to the poor, A strength to the needy in his distress, a refuge from the storm (Isaiah 25:4-5-NKJV)

In this life, we will sometimes have troubles. A storm may be a time when things aren't going our way. But no matter what, God's love for us is always there to help us overcome.

Late one afternoon, the sky turns very gray; it
looks like nighttime, yet it is still day.
Mommy is worried about you for sure. Are you
strong enough this storm to endure?
Darkness, rain, lightning, and thunder! She
can't help herself but to wonder.
She looks out the windows to see if you are
there. Are you nearby? Are you scared?
Then, out of the storm, Mommy hears your tweeting,
ever so loudly; your voice keeps repeating.
You're in trouble and calling Mommy, so she
runs to the window and looks in the trees.
There's no sign of you in a tree anywhere,
yet she hears you, loud and clear.
She continues to search through the window and the
rain; then all of a sudden, through one windowpane,
Mommy sees you hovering nearby on the ground—
one blue bird, drenched and afraid, but now found!

Without a care, she runs outside, holds out
her hand, and you jump inside!
Both of you are soaking from the driving rain and
both of you are happy to be inside again.
She dries you gently, saying, "Hello, blue." She
was glad she was here to rescue you.
You're both happy, dry, warm and at peace; you
can now rest till the storm has ceased.
Soon enough the storm goes away; the sky is
blue again, the sun, a gold display.
Birds are back and flying above; it's time for
you Petite to return to your true love.
Other birds, the sky and the trees; get on
back to the birds and the bees.

Mommy opens the door, you fly out
with a big "wahoo", forgetting this latest
venture, you've just been through.
You keep growing stronger every day, and there's no
longer any storm that can frighten this blue jay!
Now, just like the others, you are full grown,
and the world outside is your only home.
You need no one, nothing, Petite; and you
cocky girl no longer need Mommy!

Out the window and Into the rainbow!

As a sign of this everlasting covenant which I am making with you and with all living beings, I am putting my bow in the clouds. It will be the sign of my covenant with the world. Whenever I cover the sky with clouds and the rainbow appears, I will remember my promise to you and to all the animals that a flood will never again destroy all creation. (Genesis 9:12-15-ICB)

Chapter 8

Au Revoir Little Bird Blue

Mommy can no longer remember the exact day that came,
the day you didn't come when she called your name.
She'll always wonder where you did go, but you
flew away, and she saw you no more.
You never woke her again to say hi, to
grab some fruit as you flew by.
She sits in her chair in the yard some days and
longs to see you, her sweet blue jay.
She says in her heart, "Please come again—I miss you,
I do. Come peck my Bible; come peck my shoe."
If only she could hold you once more in her hand,
pet your little head, and kiss you again.
But she believes you're happy out there, with a
family of blue jays in a tree somewhere.
Perhaps you have a nest with babies inside?

She wonders, "do you ever remember
when you fell and almost died?"
But Mommy came and rescued you,
and my, did you have fun.
You played and laughed and loved each
other under God's golden sun.
Of course you don't remember a
thing; after all, that can't be so.
But that makes Mommy happy for you, sweet
friend; for your happiness, you know,
Is more important to her than anything,
and she knew someday you'd go.
It's what she wants for you, Petite, and
all the days and times you'd meet
are a gift from God, she'll always believe. So your
parting from her she does gladly but sadly receive.
To some it may sound silly, she knows, but
she still hopes it's true—that as she arrives in
heaven someday, Sweet Petite, she will see you.
You'll come flying and tweeting so loudly, just
like you used to do; you'll probably land right
on her head, and she'll laugh if you do!
And together with all her loved ones you'll
be and enjoy each other again. Mommy, the
Lord, her family, and Sweet Petite, her friend.

When I consider Your heavens, the work of Your hands,
the moon and the stars, which You have set in place;
You have your children rule over the works of Your hands;
all the animals of the field, the birds of the sky,
and the fish of the sea...LORD, our Lord, How
majestic is Your name in all the earth!

To You I lift up my eyes, O You who are enthroned
in the heavens...(Psalm 123:1-NKJV)

And say, "thank you Lord. Love, Mommy"

Printed in the USA
CPSIA information can be obtained
at www.ICGtesting.com
LVHW061737280524
781290LV00018B/299

9 798385 014446